Enjoy The Day, This Way!

~

Patricia Wynn-Mason

Copyright © 2025

ALL RIGHTS RESERVED

Published in the United States by Pen Legacy Publishing
An imprint of Pen Legacy, LLC, Pennsylvania
www.penlegacy.com

Library of Congress Cataloging-in-Publication Data has been applied for.

Paperback ISBN: 979-8-218-65528-0

PRINTED IN THE UNITED STATES OF AMERICA.

FIRST EDITION

Table of Contents

Enjoy The Day Mondays! 7

Enjoy The DayTuesdays! 19

Enjoy The Day Wednesdays! 33

Enjoy The Day Thursdays! 47

Enjoy The Day Fridays! 59

Enjoy The Day Saturdays! 71

Enjoy The Day Sundays! 79

Fruit Of The Spirit Message Series 91

Psalm 27 Message Series 95

Holidays, Special Days And Events 103

Holiday Season, New Year, Good Friday, And Resurrection Sunday 107

Good Friday And Resurrection Sunday 117

A Glimpse Of Black History Contributions And Quotes Series, Along With Valentine's Day Messages 119

Wise Words From Black Greek Letter Sorority And Fraternity Members Of The Divine Nine 128

About the Author 132

Appendix 134

Introduction

Imagine waking up each morning with a heart full of hope and an unwavering belief that today will be a good day. Picture a day where every moment is a new opportunity to see the beauty in life, extend kindness, embrace love, and live with purpose. I invite you to experience this kind of day in *Enjoy The Day, This Way* – a journey of daily inspiration that transforms the ordinary into the extraordinary.

From the first light of dawn to the peaceful rest at night, each day offers a chance to connect with something greater, to find joy in the simple things, and to trust that even in our challenges, there is a divine plan at work. Let the words in this book resonate with a deep spiritual wisdom, reminding us that we are not alone, that every day is a gift, and that our lives are part of a beautiful tapestry woven by the Creator.

This book started as providing daily inspiration for family and friends. However, it is more than just a collection of motivational messages; it is a companion for those who seek to live fully, love deeply, and walk faithfully. Whether you are facing a challenging Monday or a triumphant Tuesday, you will find in these pages the encouragement you need to rise above, press forward, and embrace the day with a heart full of gratitude and a spirit ready to soar.

So, turn the page, let these words wash over you, and prepare to embark on a daily adventure that will uplift your soul, renew your mind, and inspire you to enjoy the day—every day—this way!

Love, Patricia

ENJOY THE DAY, THIS WAY!

Enjoy The Day

Mondays!

My, My, My, My, My, My, My Monday!

Sometimes, things happen in our lives that take us by surprise, force us to regroup, and cause our hearts to feel something we've never felt before. In those times, know that God is never caught off guard. He's always in control, orchestrating His plan for us. Our "my, my" life occurrences are when He reveals Himself strong with, "I will get you by" supernatural deliverances. Enjoy the day!

Miracles From Heaven Monday!

> *1 Corinthians 2:9 — "Eyes have not seen, nor ears heard, nor has it entered into the heart of man the things which God has prepared for those who love Him."*

The mere thought of Him preparing MORE for those who love Him, should set our souls afire with so much excitement and anticipation that we cannot help but to – enjoy the day!

Missing You Monday!

Time truly does heal all wounds when we focus on unconditional love instead of unforgiving hurts. The weight and stress of holding onto pain are like poison flowing through our veins. The choice to let go and let God is like a blood transfusion that cleanses our systems and forces us to bleed His #1 condition – love. Reach out and touch someone you've been missing because of past hurts, and trust that the healing spirit of forgiveness will help you both enjoy the day!

Musical Monday!

The rhythms, beats, harmonies, flows, and synchronization are part of music's universal vibes and melodies that move us in different ways. Some tunes are playful, sensual, soothing, mystical, melancholy, or spiritually and soulfully uplifting. Whatever escape you need, music can provide. Make time to indulge yourself today by taking a musical mental vacation. It will help you enjoy the day!

Marvelous Monday!

Today, you are the sunshine. So, let the rays shine through your smile and words, as you enjoy the day!

Miracles And Mistakes Monday!

We make mistakes; God makes miracles. However, a mistake can become your miracle. How, you ask? Because ALL things work together for good to those who love God and are called according to His purpose. Enjoy the day!

Merciful Monday!

Being caring, forgiving, and gentle toward others benefits our well-being and theirs. After all, look at how God's mercy (His caring, forgiveness, compassion, kindness, and gentleness) has worked in our lives! Enjoy the day!

Mighty Good Monday!

Subscribe not to the world's mentality of the dreaded Monday morning blues, for every day with Jesus is sweeter than the day before. That's mighty good news. Enjoy the day!

Merciful Monday!

His mercy is the reason we all got another chance…and another, and another, and another. Hallelujah! Let us extend that same mercy to others who need a "one more time" chance. Enjoy the day and show mercy!

ENJOY THE DAY, THIS WAY!

Maaahhh-velous Monday!

If you are reading this message, it means God woke you up another day. It was not of your own power, it was the Lord's doing, and each new day is marvelous in our eyes. Be blessed and enjoy the day!

Magnanimous Monday!

Forgive others without resentment as you have been forgiven with unconditional love. Enjoy the day!

More Than Meets The Eye Monday!

Show people that what's inside of you is greater than what they see on the outside. Likewise, let's not judge others by their covers. Man looks at what is visible. God looks at the heart; let us do the same. Enjoy the day!

Matchless Monday!

God's words, works, and ways are undefeated, and you're on His team. So, no matter what you're going through or what it looks like, His plan is your victory. Enjoy the day!

Mistake Me Not Monday!

If it looks like, walks like, and talks like a duck, it's a duck! When people show you who they are, believe them. But beware of the wolf in sheep's clothing. As for us, let there be no mistaken identity. Let's look like, walk like, and talk like who we claim to be in Him. Enjoy the day!

Make It Happen Monday!

God doesn't call the qualified; He qualifies the called. Pay attention to the call; don't ignore it. Take the leap with faith and watch Him do a new thing in you. The first step is the hardest. But, when you do it, you'll be on your way to enjoying the day!

Me For You And You For Me Monday!

Romans 12:15 — "Rejoice with those who rejoice; weep with those who weep."

Some support requires nothing more than being there in spirit and prayer. Let others know you care and enjoy the day!

ENJOY THE DAY, THIS WAY!

Mirror, Mirror On The Wall Monday!

Who are you going to believe, the reflection or your lying eyes? If there's something you say, do, or see that you want to change about yourself, do it. If it's something that absolutely cannot be changed, embrace it. And if it's something you simply don't want to change, so be it…just know the long-term consequences. Be true to God and yourself, and you will enjoy the day!

Mo' Betta Monday!

From sunrise to sunset, may today get better and better. And before the day ends, may you find time to thank Him more and more—just because. Enjoy the day!

Monday Matters!

Oh, dear, what could the matter be? Whatever it is, God has the answer, for there is nothing new that He hasn't seen nor anything too big or hard that He can't solve. Fret not, know that He has you, and enjoy the day!

Make It Happen Monday!

I got the power! Yes, we do! The power is with us and within us. We can speak positives or negatives over our situations, for life and death are in the power of the tongue. Speak life, believe it will happen, and His will be done as you enjoy the day!

Memorable Moments Monday!

If you need a pick-me-up from the doldrums of life, be comforted and lifted with a "blast from the past" thought that warms your soul. Pause, ponder, smile...and enjoy the day!

Maybe Tomorrow Monday!

Uh, how about today? Yes, get started today. If you believe in it, then put your faith to work, because faith without works is dead. Your actions will help you enjoy the day!

Monday's Mission!

Unfinished business and loose ends cause us to trip and slip. Unforgiveness is unfinished business. Forgive someone or ask to be forgiven so the doors of hurt feelings may be closed to open doors for healing. The mission is always forgiveness and unconditional love. Apply this and enjoy the day!

Mellow Monday!

Take it easy, be light and breezy, and enjoy the day!

Make A Difference Monday!

Praise God that He isn't in the cloning business. We each have unique gifts, skills, and talents to serve others. We are different to make a difference. Bless someone today with the special quality you possess. It may be the only God-like encounter to help them enjoy the day!

Mission Never Impossible Monday!

Matthew 19:26 — *"…but with God, all things are possible."*

Many of us have something we're working on or want to do and accomplish. May this scripture from the book of Matthew be your constant encouragement and reminder that the mission is possible, and the goal can be achieved. Go for it and enjoy the day!

Moody Monday!

We reap what we sow. Have an ugly attitude and feeling like you don't want to be bothered? If so, then, force yourself to share a smile, kind word, or nice gesture with everyone you encounter today. Oh, and considering the mood you're in, it may be challenging. However, the more you do it, you'll find that while your kind words and gestures uplift others, they'll also serve as the pick-me-up you need to enjoy the day!

Motivate Yourself Monday!

"If you are always trying to be normal, you will never know how amazing you can be." ~ Maya Angelou

Take a leap of faith. Step out of the ordinary and into your extraordinary by acting on and bringing to life those things you've always dreamed and believed you could do and become. If you can see it, you can be it. Transfer it from your mind to your motion, and make it happen by thrusting yourself into action. Strides toward bringing your extraordinary and your visions to fruition will help you enjoy the day!

Make The Most of It Monday!

Even when living right, sometimes you may make what seems to be the best choices for your life, only to learn that what seemed like a good thing resulted in something other than what you were expecting. But hold on – if you are living right, know that God has you in the right place at the right time. Therefore, make the most of the situation by letting Him use you. For His plans are always to prosper us, not harm us. Enjoy the day!

Makeover Monday!

Give yourself a non-surgical facelift – also known as a smile. However, take caution; the side effects are contagiously positive, spreading quickly and easily. Enjoy the day!

Mellow Monday Evening!

Here's to a sweet, peaceful slumber. Enjoy the night!

ENJOY THE DAY, THIS WAY!

Enjoy The Day

Tuesdays!

Terrific Tuesday!

Yes, it is! So, go ahead and enjoy the day!

Tell Somebody Tuesday!

Tell someone how much you appreciate them or what they do and make it a heartfelt, enjoyable day!

Tempt Me Not Tuesday!

In the words of DMX: "Y'all gonna make me lose my mind, up in here, up in here." But, wait! Bridle the tongue! Don't curse them out, verse them out, and make it a tongue-safe and enjoyable day!

Tough It Out Tuesday!

"Yea, though I walk through the valley…"

Keyword: walk. Do not pitch a tent and stay in that place! Rise up and walk or let God carry you through the storm. Just keep pressing toward your blessing and you will enjoy the day!

Trust Him Tuesday!

That's all. Enjoy the day!

Take Me Away Tuesday!

Exhale, let go of the madness of the day, rest to be refreshed for a new tomorrow, and enjoy a peaceful night of slumber!

Think About It Tuesday!

When you can't sleep at night, have you ever thought maybe it's God saying, *"We need to talk, and you now have time"*? ~ Anonymous. Sleep well…and should you awake, begin the conversation, and know that He is listening. Enjoy your slumber!

Tuesday Evening Dreamin'!

Make it a practice to end your day with positive thoughts no matter how your day went. There's always a reason to be thankful. Say a little prayer, dream a little dream, and may you be awakened tomorrow by yet another touch of His gift of life. Enjoy the night!

Time To Shine Tuesday!

Put forth your best not for fame, fortune, promotion, or to receive recognition from others; but do your best because God is watching. When we do our best even when no one is looking, and we do it as though a service unto the Lord, He blesses us abundantly and allows us to enjoy the fruit of our labor as we enjoy the day!

Thank God It's Tuesday!

That's right, why wait for TGIF? How about thanking Him when it's Monday, Tuesday, Wednesday, Thursday, Saturday, and Sunday, too? Hey, it's another day. He made it, we are six feet above and not below, and life for those of us in Him on this side of Heaven continues. So, go ahead – get your TGIT on, and enjoy the day!

The Thrill Is Gone Tuesday!

No, it ain't! Because when I think about Jesus, what He's done for me, when I think about Jesus, how He set me free, I could dance, dance, dance, dance, dance, dance, dance all night! Whew! That praise interruption comes courtesy of our sponsor, God. Enjoy the day along with this song: *When I Think About Jesus by Kirk Franklin and the Family https://m.youtube.com/watch?v=FK9FOy9y4d0*

Tell Somebody Tuesday!

Tell someone how much you appreciate them for who they are and/or what they do. Chances are very high that it will help them to enjoy the day!

Tickle Me Tuesday!

Why is it that we feel better after a good laugh or cry? Perhaps it's because, although they are two extremes, they provide a similar release. So, the next time you find yourself crying, or laughing yourself to tears, or shedding tears of joy, know that it's good for the soul. Enjoy the day!

Team Up Tuesday!

Want to win at the game of life on this side of Heaven? Choose a team of fools on fire for the Kingdom rather than scholars on ice. Enjoy the day!

Thankful For It Tuesday!

When we didn't walk right or talk right as citizens of the Kingdom of God, He heard our cries and saw our disgrace; still, He favored us with His sufficient grace. Let's take a moment to simply say, "Thank You, Father." Enjoy the day!

Totally Into It Tuesday!

Whatever that fire is that burns within you – that thing you want to do but never acted on or started but stopped – get back to it! Once you begin to use it, He will begin to use and bless you beyond your imagination. Dreams do come true. Enjoy the day!

Trust Him Tuesday!

Sometimes we cry out, "Lord, where are you? I need to hear from you." In those times, trust that while His voice may be silent, His touch is on you and He is with you, keeping you and moving in ways you will see in time. Keep trusting, keep believing, keep watching, keep praising, and enjoy the day!

Totally Into It Tuesday!

Ain't no half-stepping! Get off the fence! No gray, no lukewarm! Jesus went all in for us, even to death. And when He rose with all power, He completed the mission, the plan. He was totally committed, from the beginning to the end, to saving us and having a relationship with us. Be all in, it will change your life! Enjoy the day!

The Way You Do the Things You Do Tuesday!

You know what it is – you do it naturally. He gifted you with it to be a blessing wherever you go and in all you do. No limits, no excuses; He's prepared you. Work it to the fullest while you enjoy the day!

Touchdown Tuesday!

Oh, yes! On your way to the goal, you may get shoved, tackled, bruised, trampled on, spit on, or even pierced in your side; but in the end, it's a win. Game over! Enjoy the day!

Trouble Don't Last Always Tuesday!

And let all God's people say, Amen! Enjoy the day!

Things People Say Tuesday!

When people talk about you, it's a reflection of who they are; it has nothing to do with you. Pray for those in glass houses and enjoy the day!

Test It Tuesday!

Kind acts are infectious. It's the kind of bug that, if it keeps spreading, it will inevitably come back to you. Test it and see. Enjoy the day!

Tantalizing Tuesday!

Proverbs 31:30 — "Charm is deceptive, and beauty fades; but a woman who fears the Lord is to be praised."

As we mature gracefully in the love and fear of the Lord, let our charm and beauty reflect His goodness and mercy on our lives. Glory! Enjoy the day!

Treat Yourself Tuesday!

So often, we're so busy taking care of everyone and everything else that we feel guilty doing something special for ourselves. Put the guilt aside and do something special for Y-O-U. You're worth it! Enjoy the day!

Touch Them Tuesday!

A kind word, gesture, compliment, and/or show of approval are always nice things to give when working with others. Use your spirit fruit of kindness to touch someone's heart and enjoy the day!

Transformed Tuesday!

Thought about saying it; but didn't. Was going to do it; but changed my mind. Heard a voice say, "One time won't hurt". Heard God say, "Keep your mind stayed on me." Praise Him for a renewing that allows us to make sound decisions of faith and enjoy the day!

Try This Tuesday!

Try what, you ask? Forgiveness. Enjoy the day!

This Is It Tuesday!

Psalm 118:24 — This is the day that the Lord has made. We shall rejoice and be glad in it!

That verse declares what it is, who did it, and what we are to do. So, why ponder or delay the action? Today, rejoice and be glad. Once you do, you will enjoy the day!

Try It Tuesday!

Try tithing your money or your time. God says to test Him at this "…and see if I will not open the windows of Heaven and pour out so much blessing that you will not have room enough for it." Given all the other things we've tried and tested (good and bad), we should jump at the thought of God wanting us to test Him. After all, He controls the floodgates! Put Him to the test, give in some way, and enjoy the day!

Tender Tuesday!

Let your words live with tender touches of encouragement and compliments that motivate and uplift others. Excuse yourself from those who use their words to minimize, ridicule, and bring you or others down. Know what to reject and accept into your spirit. However, if you fall short, may His tender mercies be with you. Enjoy the day!

Teachable To The End Tuesday!

Psalm 92:14 —"They shall still bear fruit in old age; they shall be fresh and flourishing."

For God to do a new thing in you, be willing and open to make room for new stuff to come in, and for some old stuff to come out. No matter what your age, new things can happen. As you mature, be the old dog that can be taught new tricks. Enjoy the day!

Thankful For This Tuesday!

We will never see this day again. Record a memorable moment from today to reflect on in the future and make it an enjoyable day!

That's The Way I Feel About You Tuesday!

No condemnation; no judgement. Just as He loves us unconditionally, let us extend the same love to one another. Love so that you may be loved – unconditionally. Share this love with family, friends, and even foes, allowing them to experience His love through your actions. Enjoy the day!

Takeover Tuesday!

Train your positive thoughts to overpower any negative ones that enter your mind and try to escape through your words. Make this change a daily practice, and you'll notice a positive transformation in what you say, as well as in the people and opportunities you attract. Also, challenge yourself to see the good in others instead of focusing on their flaws. We all have qualities worth celebrating. Embrace this positive mental takeover, and you will enjoy the day!

Talk It Up Tuesday, Y'all!

Tell the people what it's all about! Whatever it is, deliver it in a way that enlightens, helps, and does not offend. If

ENJOY THE DAY, THIS WAY!

you have nothing positive or worth sharing to impart, bridal your tongue until the Lord lays some good words on your heart. Talk ain't cheap when it feeds others' words from which they may reap. Enjoy the day!

ENJOY THE DAY, THIS WAY!

Enjoy The Day

Wednesdays!

Walk This Way, Talk This Way Wednesday!

Shame the devil and tell the truth. You didn't always look like the beautiful person you are today; for the path many of us were on, did not look like it would end at the door of the Kingdom. Making the conscious decision to accept, worship, serve, and follow the Lord changed the trajectory of our walk, talk and overall being. Be thankful for the wonderful change and continue enjoying life anew in Him as you enjoy the day!

Wake Up Wednesday!

In the musical words of Teddy Pendergrass, *"It's time to start a new day."* Begin it with prayer, proceed with unconditional love free of condemnation and judgment as you step high in your sandals of peace, and end it with a heart full of gratitude! Enjoy the day!

What Y'all Want Wednesday!

What y'all people want, He's got. Everything you need, He will provide. Everything you have, He gave. Even gave His life, so you'd be saved. Sing those words to the beat of "What Ya Want" by Ruff Ryders ft. Eve, and you'll have a song to help you enjoy the day!

Wishing You Bluebirds In The Spring Wednesday!

But most of all, I wish you love. Enjoy the day!

(Those words are from a great jazz classic. Here's my favorite rendition... just a little something to lighten your day and make it smoother.)[1]

Wonderful Ways Wednesday!

When you commit to loving yourself, being yourself, and not conforming to meet others' expectations – the beautiful, incredible, and wonderful ways that God implanted in you will fully surface, shine, and blossom. Embrace who you are in Him, and you will enjoy the day!

What-A-Great-Day Wednesday!

Spring is in the air! Instead of going to the gym, try an outdoor workout routine where the fresh breeze serves as

---

[1] Gloria Lynne "I Wish You Love" (youtube.com)

nature's air conditioning to cool you off as you exercise. Take a walk, go biking, jump rope, or go for a run. Whatever you do, make it fun! Enjoy the day!

Wonderful Wednesday!

The Lord God is our Wonderful Counselor, and His wonderful counseling is mind-blowing and mind-boggling. His advice, guidance, and instruction confound the wise; yet it blesses us. So, whatever you're going through, know He has a divine plan to get you through it. Most of all, know He loves you and wants to keep you *full of His wonder*. Enjoy the day!

Whimsical Wednesday!

Be fancy-free and enjoy the day!

Want For Nothing Wednesday!

Thank Him for all that He's blessed you with, and know that He will always be Jehovah Jireh, the God who provides. Amen to that and enjoy the day!

Worship Without Worry Wednesday!

There's no shame in our Jesus game; put your hands up and praise Him! Enjoy the freedom to get your worship on as you enjoy the day!

Watch And Wait Wednesday!

Keep praying, keep watching, be still, and know that God has the answer you're waiting to receive. Enjoy the day!

Word Up Wednesday!

Bless your enemies, haters, and those who talk about you by sending a word up asking God to forgive them, for they know not what they do. Love rules! They can talk about us all they please but let us talk about them on our knees. Enjoy the day!

They're Watching Us Wednesday!

Lead by example. Let them witness the warmth of your caring heart through the touch of your kind and encouraging words. Love on them and enjoy the day!

Wow Them With Your Words Wednesday!

Show them you're the consummate package of beauty and brains. Display wisdom, speak life, exhibit love, employ charisma, and enjoy the day!

What You Want Wednesday!

God is the great "I Am." Imagine Him saying to you, *"I Am whatever you need Me to be. What you want, baby, I got it!"* And surely, He does. Seek, knock, ask—and enjoy the day!

Whine Or Win Wednesday!

Choose to win! And if you must whine – add cheese, exhale, keep your armor intact, pick up your sword (the Bible), and get back to being a soldier on purpose for the Kingdom! Enjoy the day!

Whenever, Wherever, Whatever Wednesday!

Praise God for the spirit of choice to do what we please. However, in choosing, let's be mindful and wise to do what pleases Him. Enjoy the day!

Where I Am Weak Wednesday!

Superman has Superwoman, Batman has Robin, and Oprah has Gale. Include in your life, people who complement your weaknesses with their strengths and vice versa. Enjoy the day!

Wellness Wednesday!

Do your mind, body, and soul a favor by prioritizing your health with yearly checkups. If something is ailing you, don't put it off – find out what it could be and your options. Regular doctor visits could prevent later hospitalization, surgery, or something worse. Live well while enjoying the day!

Washed Clean Wednesday!

Have a covered-in-the-blood, stain-free mind with no guilt – you've been forgiven! So, when the enemy brings up your past, you bring up his future. Enjoy the day!

What Will It Be Wednesday!

People talking versus God's words – will you believe the chatter or the latter? Choose the latter, God's word – it's infallible! Enjoy the day!

Worth It Wednesday!

"Those that don't got it, can't show it. Those that got it, can't hide it." — Zora Neale Hurston

This is true. Yet, each of us has something within that God placed there for a purpose. Identify it, tap into it, and let it be used for good. Enjoy the day!

Why, Oh, Why Wednesday!

(*Thinking out loud...*) Why are some church people some of the worst people, always criticizing and judging? *"If he doesn't pull those pants up..."; "If she doesn't cover her body up some more..."; "They better think twice before coming in my church!"* Let us be fishers of men, inviting them to come as they are instead of rejecting and throwing them back out into the world. Enjoy the day!

Willing Wednesday!

Have a willing heart, spirit, and mind to work on changing that thing you do or say that you know doesn't please God. None of us are perfect. If you don't know what it is, ask Him to reveal it to you. Enjoy the day!

Wonderfully Made Wednesday!

Let's admire and respect the unique characteristics, skills, and qualities of divine distinction that He's given each of us through His wondrous works. Never ridiculing; always uplifting. Don't hate; appreciate. Enjoy the day!

What It Looks Like Wednesday!

It looks like whatever it beholds. Hence, whatever you behold is what you will begin to look like and become. Be beautiful by beholding the fruit of the spirit and enjoy the day!

Weird And Wonderful Wednesday!

Leave an uncanny but cool message for a loved one about what they do that you like. A message posted on the mirror, a note in their lunch bag, or a voicemail that makes them smile, laugh, or even puff out their chest. Creativity is limitless when it comes to keeping love alive in our families. Make their day and enjoy yours!

Wait For It Wednesday!

Whatever it is, it's on the way. Patience is a virtue, and God's blessings are always worth the wait. Stay calm, whistle while you wait instead of grumbling, and enjoy the day!

Work On This Wednesday!

Self-control. Enjoy the day!

Work On This Wednesday!

Forgiveness. Enjoy the day!

Wrap Your Head Around This Wednesday!

When we mentally let go of some people and things, we open ourselves to new possibilities for God to show and do in us a new thing. It truly does start in the mind as to how we choose to accept and deal with that which remains but bring us no joy, just pain. Let go, let God, and enjoy the day!

Winsome Wednesday!

Believers with prune faces, shallow words, pompous attitudes, and self-righteousness can often cause those searching to think, *if that's what being saved is about, I'll pass*. To win some, we ourselves must be "winsome". Let our look of love draw them in as we enjoy the day!

Wake Up Wednesday!

If you have a dream that rests dormant within you, it's time to wake it up and bring it to life. Nothing beats a failure but a try. Hence, give it a go, and remember, dreams can come true. Enjoy the day!

Wise Wednesday!

We can be part of something while still thinking independently. Be defined by your good, not your group. When you're characterized by your positive values, it uplifts and makes the whole group look better. Mob mentality is mindless mentality. So, think for yourself, and enjoy the day!

Wishing It Was Warm Wednesday!

That's all. Enjoy the day!

Wings Of Love Wednesday!

Because the Lord holds and covers us, we can wait upon Him with renewed strength in times of need or change. On the wings of His love, we can soar like eagles, run without growing weary, and walk yet never faint. Be lifted high as you rest your wings upon His, and you will enjoy the day!

With God Or With The Mob Wednesday!

It's hard to go against the mob without ending up as an outcast. With God, you have a Father and a family who loves you unconditionally even when you act, think, look, and live differently than the rest of the family. I'll say it again: mob mentality is mindless mentality. Instead of the mob, choose the family that represents the true in-crowd, for He lives in us, and we live in Him. Walk in your coolness and stay connected to His in-crowd while you enjoy the day!

ENJOY THE DAY, THIS WAY!

Enjoy The Day

Thursdays!

Trim Thursday!

If it's fatty or something that isn't good for you, simply say, "No, thank you" and keep it moving with a nice walk around the block. Making healthy choices will help you enjoy the day!

There's A Win In You Thursday!

Be the person that people want on their team because of your positive, encouraging, and motivating attitude. If chosen to be on the team and your skills are less than great, then feel blessed and know that you were chosen because, when it comes to all things in life, your infectious energy exudes "Win!" Enjoy the day!

Touchful Thursday!

May your kind words and gestures be just the touch someone needs. Enjoy the day!

Treasure Chest Thursday!

Wear something you treasure today or serve a meal on the fine China that you treasure but never use. They are priceless, and so are you. Enjoy the day!

Turn Up Thursday!

You know that thing you do that people really like about you? Well today, put it on steroids and show 'em what you're really workin' with. Don't stop – get it, get it and enjoy the day!

Trust The Truth Thursday!

When in doubt, test the word of others by the Word of God. His Word will bring all things to light. Enjoy the day!

That's The Way, Uh-huh, I Like It Thursday!

Isn't life so much better when we pray, listen, and obey; get out of His way; continue to watch, work, and wait with expectation, then stand back in awe and wonderment as His plans for our lives come to fruition? WHOA! What a mighty God we serve! We more than like what He does for us; we love it! Likewise, let's give Him what he loves and expects from us – boisterous praise! Do that, and you will enjoy the day!

Tickle Me Thursday!

What's the word, Hummingbirds? Share a story or joke with someone to help lighten up your day and theirs with a smile and laughter. Enjoy the day!

Talking Square Biz Thursday, Y'all!

Say what you mean and mean what you say, let your yes be yes and your nay be nay. Skirting around issues, beating around the bush, vague answers, lies, and lack of communication only build confusion, which can result in years of misunderstanding causing good relationships to sour. Sharing stories, pictures, and parables to get one's point across is fine. However, be direct, not dissecting; honest, not hurtful; human, not high above; open, not deceiving; and kind, not cruel with your words – setting the standard for others to do the same. Enjoy the day!

Take It To The Head Thursday!

Whatever it is, take it to the Father; He knows what's best. Instead of bending your elbow and taking it to the lips, bend your knees and take it to the three's—the Father, Savior, and Holy Spirit. Enjoy the day!

Thunderous Thursday!

May the electrifying gifts you possess be the "boom" to ignite a spark of hope in someone who is lost. Let the thunder of your light break through the deafening sounds that speak no hope, and like lightning, may it light the path for them that leads to Him who is the Truth, the Way, and the Life. Boom, Boom! Enjoy the day!

Thirsty Thursday!

As we hydrate our bodies with fluids, let us be mindful to hydrate our spirits with the Living Word so that we may thirst no more. Enjoy the day!

Thoughtful Thursday!

If someone enters your thoughts today, give them a call. It will make your day and theirs. Enjoy the day!

Tickle Me Thursday!

Laughter is the goal, and it's good for the soul! So, make 'em smile, make 'em laugh – and just think, it may help someone get their joy back. Enjoy the day!

Truly Thankful Thursday!

So, He didn't give you what you wanted, but surely, He supplied your need. For this, be thankful, and enjoy the day!

Therapeutic Thursday!

That's what great weather is – therapeutic…and we all know everybody loves the sunshine. So, go outside and soak up some rays while enjoying the day!

Tear The Roof Off Thursday!

Have some "by any means necessary" people in your life who are ready, willing, and able to do what looks crazy, bizarre, and extraordinary to everyone but God when it comes to getting your blessing. Some say choose fools on fire versus scholars on ice. However, there are scholars on fire who are ready and willing to tear the roof off to get to the blessing, as well. Choose your cohorts wisely and enjoy the day!

Touch Someone Thursday!

Reach out to someone you haven't heard from in a while and let them know they were on your mind. We all like to be remembered. Enjoy the day!

Turnaround Thursday!

Whatever it is, know that you have choices and change is constant. However, if God doesn't change the situation, He'll bring about a wonderful change in you that will help you make it through. Enjoy the day!

Togetherness Thursday!

Being on one accord, of the same mind toward the goal, and having the same passion – now that's a good recipe for getting the job done. Enjoy the day!

Treasure The Moments Thursday!

Create an unforgettable moment for someone you've forgotten about or lost touch with and make it a time you both will remember! Enjoy the day!

To The Next Level Thursday!

After "I did it", should come "What's next, Lord?" He ain't through with you yet, and there's always room to grow and be used in the Kingdom. Let Him take you higher and enjoy the day!

Take It Away Thursday!

Sometimes, God just wants us to be still. And in those times, He'll show Himself so strong that His greatness will take our breath away. Exhale, know that He is God, and enjoy the day!

Tell Him About It Thursday!

Not everything is meant for everyone, and not everyone is equipped to understand the unique tests and trials God has placed in your life. Some experiences are deeply personal and best kept between you and Him. Trust that Him knowing is enough. Enjoy the day!

Think Back And Be Thankful Thursday!

"When I was a child, I spoke as a child, I understood as a child, I thought as a child. But when I became a man (when I became whole in Him), I put away childish ways." — 1 Cor. 13:11

We all have things we did that we no longer do, thanks to the change that came when we chose God and drew nearer to Him. Truth be told, some of us still have ways that resemble childlike behavior. Today, commit to living in a way that reflects who we are meant to be in Him. Enjoy the day!

Thankful For Them Thursday!

Family—can't live without them, can't live with them, can't kill them. Friends—some are for life, some for a season, and some for a reason. As for the others, know when to hold 'em, fold 'em, walk away, or run. Thank God for the purpose of relationships – the good, the bad, and the ugly. Enjoy the day!

Tip It In Thursday!

Some things may need an extra touch or push to complete the move. If you want it and know it's worth it, touch it again, but this time, score a move for yourself by finishing the job. Now that's some slam-dunk advice to help you enjoy the day!

"That's It" Thursday!

Still trying to figure out what you're called to do or how you can be a blessing to others and the Kingdom? Stop trying to figure it out and begin doing something that you like or have thought about doing. God can make you effective wherever you use your efforts for the good. That's it – now the secret is out. Enjoy the day!

Tell Him, Trust Him Thursday!

I had a talk with my Savior last night. He reassured me everything would be all right. Prayer and communication with God help us to enjoy the day!

Think On This Thursday!

"When the solution is simple, God is answering." — Albert Einstein.

God does not complicate things; we do. Fret not, stress less – the answer you seek is coming. Get out of His way.

However, while awaiting His answer, continue to live, for life goes on. Enjoy the day!

Thankful For Reminders Of His Protection Thursday!

No weapon formed against us shall prosper.

The Lord is the strength of our lives; of whom shall we be afraid?

God is our refuge and strength, a very present help in times of trouble.

Let's praise and thank God for His "blocking" power that kept and protected us from what could have happened. When we think about the times He did block something, may a praise rise up in each of our spirits that forces us to enjoy the day!

ENJOY THE DAY, THIS WAY!

Enjoy The Day

Fridays!

Freely Thinking Friday!

"Happiness is the absence of striving for happiness."

— *Anonymous*

Enjoy the day!

Fire Back Friday!

When the enemy uses you as target practice, fire back with the weapon that makes demons tremble, flee, and fall – the Word of God. Enjoy the day!

Forget About It, Dismiss It, And Rebuke It Friday!

Let go of those things the enemy tries to plant in your mind that cause you to doubt yourself, and most of all, are contrary to what God says about you. Satan's power to kill, steal, and destroy our dreams only works when we forget who our powers are—God the Creator, Savior, and Comforter. In them lies your strength to defeat every foe. Be empowered knowing who your Kingdom powers are, and you will enjoy the day!

Fresh Start Friday!

His mercies are new every day! Enjoy the day!

Forget-Me-Not Friday!

Some people live by the principle – out of sight, out of mind. Now, in some instances, that may be necessary, and God may have closed the door permanently. But, if that's not the case, and God lays someone on your mind, heart, or spirit, give them a call and let them know they're not forgotten. I said it once and I'll say it again, we all like to be remembered. Enjoy the day!

Force Yourself Friday!

Stay the course, stick with the plan, go the extra mile, walk away, ignore the tempter, slay the words of naysayers with the words that God says...and keep pressing toward the prize! Enjoy the day!

Fearless First Steps Friday!

Myles Munroe once said, "The wealthiest place on the planet is just down the road. It is the cemetery. There lie buried companies that were never started, inventions that were never made, bestselling books that were never written, and masterpieces that were never painted. In the cemetery is buried the greatest treasure of untapped potential." Oftentimes, fear is the reason people take their dreams with them. Let that not be you. Overcome fear and doubt by taking the first steps. God can turn our baby steps into leaps and bounds…He just needs us to make that first move toward the dream, the prize. You've thought about it long enough; now be about it and enjoy the day!

Fun Is For All Friday!

Go out and be amongst the many variations of God's children and experience His wonderful works in the multitude of beautiful places and spaces He has created for our pleasure. Relish the moments and enjoy the day!

So Fresh And So Clean Friday!

Wear something you know you look fly in and enjoy the day!

Fitness For Freedom Friday!

Set the mind, body, and soul free by treating the dis-ease in your life with a fitness reprieve from it all. Walk, jog, run, swim, yoga, Pilates, spin class, dance – whatever your fitness relief, just do it and enjoy the day!

Fortunate Friday!

Feel fortunate for the different people, relationships, and personalities in your life whom you can go to when you need to talk, cry, pray, laugh, vent, get away, chill, etcetera. And remember, just as you're fortunate to have them, they're fortunate to have you. Enjoy the day!

Let It Flow Friday!

Whatever it is – let it flow. That outfit that catches the breeze, your new hairstyle – just let them flow. Most of all, try letting your worries flow right out of your mind…the goal is to enjoy the day!

Fresh And Fly Friday!

Whether you're dressing for success, a stroll on the beach, a walk in the park, or going out partying, wear something that makes you feel like a million bucks on the inside and the outside. And remember, you can be appealing even if it's somewhat revealing; however, leave a little to the imagination as you enjoy the day!

Free From Fear Friday!

Sometimes, God will put us face-to-face with something we fear or would never expect to go through. When this happens, know that God is with you; and when we stay in Him, giants fall, and walls come down! Fear not and enjoy the day!

Fashioned For Favor Friday!

Our Lord and Tailor cuts us from His fabric, shapes and designs us for His use, and favors us for our obedience. His style is always in season. Wear it well and enjoy the day!

Flying High Friday!

Let your smile hit 'em; let your beauty take control – your inner beauty – the joy, peace, and love inside you. It's all contagious, just like your smile. Stay up and enjoy the day!

Found Friday!

Let's love on those who are lost and trying to find their way. Talk to them; pray for them. No judging, no shutting them out – we all have a past. I once was blind, but now I see... Enjoy the day!

Fit For A King/Queen Friday!

If you have yours already, praise God! However, for the rest of us singles – if you want one, trust that God is preparing your life partner for you as He's preparing you for them. Get excited with expectation for what's to come as you enjoy the day!

Fashionable Friday!

Whatever you're doing or wherever you're going—whether you're dressing up or down, keep it fresh, keep it fly, wear it boldly, and don't be shy. Enjoy the day!

Food For The Fight Friday!

Whatever you feed your spirit most is what's going to elevate in the battle. If you want to win, feed your spirit daily with the word of God, for the weapons of our warfare are not carnal. Enjoy the day!

Free To Get High Friday!

Lecrae and Mali Music sang, "I tried getting high, but it left me low." Me, too. How about you? Let us get lifted high, high with praise and worship to God, who takes us on a natural high as we continue to fly high in Him during the highs and lows of life. So, go ahead, feel free to get your high on—that natural, everlasting high – and enjoy the day!

Feelin' It Friday!

Peace that surpasses all understanding; joy, joy, unspeakable joy; and love that forgives – be filled with these three things, pass the feeling on, and enjoy the day!

Fo' Sho' Friday!

Superstition ain't the way! We are blessed and highly favored. It has nothing to do with good or bad luck. It has everything to do with our Father who opens doors for us that no one can close and closes doors in our lives that no one can open. Know for sure, that your blessings, favor, trials, and tribulations are not by chance, but are part of the plan to help you enjoy your day, and ultimately, your life!

Fortunate Friday!

How many times and how many ways has God blessed us? If we could count the times and the ways, we would find that our lists are infinite and continue to grow. He's faithful, He's fair; and for that, we're fortunate. So, whenever you can't sleep, don't count sheep; instead, count your blessings…they're endless! Enjoy the day!

First Things First Friday!

Pray. Enjoy the day!

Forward Friday!

The beauty of each chapter in our lives is that God gives us a beginning, middle, and an end. Some chapters come with hard times and sorrow; others are filled with enchantment and bliss. The main thing is to avoid getting stuck in one chapter – even if it feels super good. If you're stuck, force yourself to turn the page; it's the only way to get to what God has for you in the next chapter of your life. Remove the bookmark and enjoy the day!

For Real Friday!

Jesus is real for real, and He wants to have a real relationship with each of us. Spend time with Him daily; and remember, He knows you better than you know yourself. So, keep it real that He may draw nearer to you, as you draw nearer to Him. Enjoy the day!

Fine, So Fine Friday!

As we walk and grow in Him, that's how He makes us look on both, the inside and the outside – fine, so fine! It's represented in our walk, talk, serving, giving, sharing, caring, learning, living, and unconditional love for others. True, we still have some rough edges that need smoothing out. However, let the refined that He's already defined stand out, as you enjoy the day!

Fit Friday!

Accept the fact that healthy eating and exercise are a daily plan for life. Junk in, junk out – I'm tryna tell you what it's all about! It ain't hard to give up the lard and do some work in the yard. Use less butter and jelly, and do some sit-ups for the belly. It may sound funny, but it's true; healthy living is what's best for me and you. Enjoy the day!

Forever Hopeful And Prayerful Friday!

Whatever you're hoping and believing for yourself or someone else, keep trusting that it will happen. With

God, all things are possible. Expect the best and prepare for all possibilities. Whatever the outcome, His will be done. Enjoy the day!

Fantastic Fall Friday!

Enjoy the day!

Forever With You Friday!

The Lord said He would never leave you nor forsake you; believe Him, for He doesn't lie. Therefore, in all things, know that you are never alone; with Him, you're in the best company possible; and in Him, you'll have peace that surpasses all understanding when life happens. Enjoy the day!

ENJOY THE DAY, THIS WAY!

Enjoy The Day

Saturdays!

Satisfaction Saturday!

What do people mean when they say, "I can't get no satisfaction"? Well, yes, you can, because when the Lord opens His hand, He satisfies the desire of every living thing – Psalm 145:16. Connect with Him, get yourself some satisfaction, and you will enjoy the day!

Sensational Saturday!

Maximize and enjoy the day!

It's Singing Saturday!

Put on some music while driving; sing out loud or groove in your seat like no one is watching! As soon as the light turns, you'll be cruising off. Let the drivers pass you by, but not life. Have fun on the road, be safe, and enjoy the day!

Say It Like You Feel It Saturday!

And remember to add the fruit of "goodness" to your words so no one walks away hurt. Enjoy the day!

Selfishly Sweet Saturday!

Take at least one hour to have some sweet time with yourself and enjoy the day!

Serene Saturday!

Keep it mellow as you enjoy the day!

Smooth Saturday!

Take time to bask in the quiet moments, and make it an enjoyable, smooth day!

Sensational Saturday!

It's not just a look, it's a feeling. So, let the "sensational you" shine on the inside and the outside as you enjoy the day!

Simply Said Saturday!

"Funny how we call God our Father and Jesus our brother but find it hard to introduce them to our family and friends." – *Anonymous*

Hmmm… Enjoy the day!

Still Small Voice Saturday!

When we quiet our agendas, we'll hear His. Hush, listen, obey – a perfect trifecta to help you enjoy the day!

Smiling Faces Saturday!

Yup, some smiling faces do tell lies. But let our smiles be genuine, infectious, and representative of the light inside us because of the living God who dwells within us. He is the Truth. Invite Him in, begin to smile, and enjoy the day!

Slumber Time Saturday!

And He will give His children rest… Good night and enjoy your sleep!

Simply Said Saturday!

He's able…and therefore, so are you. Enjoy the day!

Simply Said Saturday!

He lives! Enjoy the day!

Saying What His Word Says Saturday!

"*For we walk by faith, not by sight.*" 2 Corinthians 5:7

Enjoy the day!

Seeing Saturday!

God's awesomeness is everywhere! Just look around you. There it is – yup, that's His awesomeness helping you to enjoy the day!

Simply Said Saturday!

Enjoy the day!

Sane And Sure Saturday!

The enemy is the master of confusion. God isn't confused or fickle, nor should we be. Decide today to walk in your power of love, peace, and a sound mind, and you will enjoy the day!

Saying What The Word Says Saturday!

"Love prospers when fault is forgiven, but dwelling on it separates close friends." Proverbs 17:9

Enjoy the day!

So-And-So, Such-And-Such Saturday!

Fill in the blanks: "Lord, please bless (so-and-so) that he/she/they may (such-and-such). Amen." Now, whomever the so-and-so is that you prayed for, we all touch and agree with you that such-and-such will happen. And let all the people of God say, "Amen!" Enjoy the day!

Share This Saturday!

A smile. Enjoy the day!

Somebody Said It Saturday!

Give God what's right, not what's left. Enjoy the day!

Saying What The Word Says Saturday!

"Every good and perfect gift is from above." James 1:17

Enjoy the day!

Some Nice Words To Say Saturday!

"Please" and "Thank you" are winning words that really do go a long way. Try using them more often and enjoy the day!

Solitary Moments Saturday!

There will always be things to do. Take some time for yourself. Literally, chill and enjoy the first Saturday of the new year!

Soulful Saturday!

Listen to some good music and eat healthy food that's good for the body and soul. Most of all, enjoy the day!

Saying What The Word Says Saturday!

"He who guards his mouth and tongue guards his soul from troubles." — *Proverbs 21:23*

Know when to seal those lips and enjoy the day!

Share Something Saturday!

Share a joke, a laugh, a meal, a hug, a good word, or just a moment with someone. It will help you both enjoy the day!

ENJOY THE DAY, THIS WAY!

Enjoy The Day

Sundays!

Soulful Sunday!

Join in with a clap, praise wave, or a "Hallelujah" when the choir sings a song that moves your soul. Embrace the music and enjoy the day!

Speak And See Yourself As A Kingdom Citizen Sunday!

It's been said that the Kingdom does not have sick people trying to get healthy; we are healthy people fighting off sickness. Likewise, in the Kingdom, there are no poor people trying to get wealthy; we are wealthy people fighting off poverty! No Jesus; know lack! Know Jesus; no lack! Enjoy the day!

Shine On Sunday!

This little light of mine, I'm gonna let it shine. You do the same and enjoy the day!

Soul Searching Sunday!

At different points in our lives, certain scriptures will minister to our spirits more profoundly and significantly than they did in prior times. That's because life happens, and change does come. And while positive change is always good, it can often rock the very core of our souls when we must readjust our worlds to accommodate an unwelcome change. Breathe. Search your mind and soul. You didn't see it coming, but He did, and His plans are intentional and for our good. God is in control, and with Him, so are we. Enjoy the day!

Straight Talk Sunday!

Be ye not concerned about making it onto someone's A-list, B-list, or C-list. Just make sure you're on the G-list (God's list)! God has one list, and He wants all our names to be on the roll. There is no other list that matters. For anyone who doesn't choose Him, He gives one other option: "Go to Hell." Choose to be on His list, and you will enjoy the day, and eternity with Him!

Search Your Heart Before Speaking Your Mind Sunday!

Whatever your heart is filled with will come out of your mouth. Hence, think twice if it's not nice. Enjoy the day!

It's Sho' Nuff Sunday Morning!

Whatever your plans are today, take time to gracefully raise your hand and give God a praise wave of thanks for another day on this side of Heaven. Life is a gift from God...someone needs to know that today. Enjoy life and the day!

Soak It In Sunday!

Take time to relax, tune in, and bask in all God has blessed us with by using all your senses. Taste, smell, hear, see, and feel the beauty and greatness of everything we take for granted – the colorful scenery, the ocean sounds, the touch of a kiss or loved one's hand. Enjoy the day!

Shout Now Sunday!

Be your own cheering section – praising and worshipping as you watch and wait for your next spiritual blessing, breakthrough, or miracle to turn the bend and meet you at the finish line called *Rejoice*. Enjoy the day!

Strong Sunday!

The strength of the Lord is our help, and He provides it in many ways. So, let the weak say, "I am strong." Let the strong say, "You ain't heavy – you're my sister, my brother, my friend." And let all the people resoundingly say, "Amen!" Enjoy the day!

Set It Off Sunday!

When you think about what God has brought you through or removed you from to get you to where you are today, it's okay to "set it off" with a happy dance or tears of joy…He had you all the time! Enjoy the day!

Sovereign Sunday!

Let us decrease so that He who sits high and looks low may increase and show Himself strong in our lives. The joy of the Lord is our strength. Enjoy the day!

Silent Night Sunday!

Here's to a peaceful night of sweet slumber. Enjoy!

Sensational Sunday!

You know what to do…praise Him for being just who He is – God all by Himself! Glory Hallelujah! Enjoy the day!

Something About Sunday!

In His infinite wisdom, God set aside a day where we may rest from work to have fellowship with family and friends while breaking bread and spending quality time in His name. Good God, what a Master Planner! Enjoy the day!

Super Fly Sunday!

Wear that retro outfit you look good in or rock that hairstyle from back in the day while keeping your mind, body, and soul in Him who brought us from then to now. Enjoy the day!

Saving Grace Sunday!

God draws us to His light, removes us from dark places, places us in darkrooms where He turns negatives into beautiful pictures, and then presents us to the world for us to tell others about Him who made us new. Jesus saves...tell somebody and enjoy the day!

Saturate Us Sunday!

You know what each of us needs; so, pour it on us, Lord, that we may be awoken, restored, and renewed in freshness and fullness with the dawn of each new morning. Amen. Enjoy the day!

Support When We Stumble Sunday!

"Though we may fall, we shall not be utterly cast down; for the Lord upholds us with His hand."

— *Psalm 37:24*

Be not ashamed when you stumble. Be encouraged to return and continue the path He has you on. In doing so, the falls and stumbles will be less and less. Still covered, keep stepping, and enjoy the day!

Serendipity Sunday!

Count it all joy when things turn around for your good. Moreover, be mindful to give God the credit, for luck has nothing to do with it. Only He can use enemies as agents to get His work done. Remember, ALL things work together for our well-being and favor. Enjoy the day!

Stand On This Sunday!

The Word. Enjoy the day!

Surround Sound Sunday!

When God gives life to anyone or anything, He also gives it a sound. Some sounds are more audible than others, and all the sounds together create a universal vibration. This universal vibration is often referred to as "Om". However, I believe it to be the surround sound of life, and the central station is God. When we stay tuned to Him, we will know which signals and frequencies to block or receive. Adjust your spiritual antennas to WGOD, turn up the volume, and enjoy the day!

Surrounded Sunday!

It's here, it's there, it's everywhere – the omnipresent, omnipotent, omniscient spirit of God. It fills all time and space since before the beginning of existence through eternity. The magnitude and fullness of His Absolute Being is so unimaginably great, He told Moses, "You cannot see My face, for no man shall see Me and live." Until we can behold the all-in-all of His glory face-to-face in Heaven, He surrounds us with His spirit that we may feel, taste, see, smell, hear, know, and be assured that we are never alone. Glory Hallelujah, Amen, and Good God! Enjoy the day!

"Say Whaaaaat" Sunday!

I heard someone say, "It doesn't take all that dancing and shouting." Puh-leez! If I feel like bustin' loose and getting my praise on – step aside! You don't know like I know what He's done for me! Out! Feel free to be free and enjoy the day!

Sunday's Best!

Let's be our best for others we encounter today. Yes, let's display the best personality and overall best disposition. For, not only are the eyes of others on us, God is always watching. Be pleasing in His sight and theirs as you enjoy the day!

Sunset Sunday!

Always make amends with loved ones before the day ends, for the word of God says, "Be angry and do not sin. Don't let the sun go down on your wrath..." Going to bed with grudges, anger, and bitterness, hinders us from entering peaceful slumber. However, He promised that He will give His children rest. Apologize, forgive, or do whatever is in order, and you will enjoy the night!

So Far, So Good Sunday!

Milestones are accomplishments. Be it the length of time with your mate, how long you've been on your job, or the time you've put in thus far toward any goal you're working to achieve – feel good about how far you've come. Praise God for endurance, pat yourself on the back, and enjoy the day!

Stay In Shape Sunday!

Eat daily from the word of God that the spirit and soul may be fed and nourished throughout the marathon of life. Enjoy the day!

Silent Sunday!

Hopefully, we all had an enjoyable day, and may we also enjoy a peaceful slumber. Goodnight.

Saturday/Sunday Weekend Reminder Of Whose We Are!

"Fear not, for I have redeemed you; I have called you by name; you are Mine. When you pass through the waters, I will be with you; and through the rivers, they shall not overflow you. When you walk through the fire, you shall not be burned, nor shall the flame scorch you. For I am the Lord your God...fear not, for I am with you." – Isaiah 43:1-3

Praise God for His blessed assurance and enjoy the weekend!

ENJOY THE DAY, THIS WAY!

Fruit Of The Spirit

Message Series

Mindful Monday!

Be mindful of the fruit of the spirit – **love, peace, patience, joy, kindness, goodness, faithfulness, gentleness**, and **self-control**. Apply these and you will enjoy the day!

Think On This Tuesday!

Let's think about the fruit of self-control by applying it throughout the day (everyday). Our Lord demonstrated and gave us the ultimate picture of this fruit throughout the Living Word. Hence, in Him, we can learn to manage our actions, feelings, and emotions when tempted (even when we want to cut someone's ear off. Put the knife down, Peter! ☺) Therefore, follow the lead of our Savior, let the fruit of *self-control* develop in your spirit, and you will enjoy the day!

Warm Wednesday!

Aaaahhh – *kindness* and *gentleness* – two spirit fruit that help bring out the warmth in others. Test it and see for yourself. Meanwhile, enjoy the day!

Thankful Thursday!

Thankful for the fruit of *faithfulness* which allows us to be true to ourselves and loyal to the people and things in which we believe. Trust God, be faithful, and you will enjoy the day!

Fill Me Up Friday!

May you be filled with the fruit of *patience* to maintain the fruit of *peace* so no one may steal your spirit fruit of *joy*. Enjoy the day!

Say It Like You Feel It Saturday!

However, remember to add the fruit of *goodness* to your words so no one walks away hurt. Enjoy the day!

Surrender It All Sunday!

That's what Christ did for us at Calvary, that He may rise with all power! Now that's *love* – the greatest of all the spirit fruit. Give up something to get something greater, share the love, and you will enjoy the day!

ENJOY THE DAY, THIS WAY!

Psalm 27

Message Series

Sure, Supersedes Scared Saturday!

Psalm 27:1 – "The Lord is my light and my salvation, of whom shall I fear?"

Nothing and no one. We aren't scared; we're prepared! Enjoy the day!

Strong Sunday!

Psalm 27:1 – "The Lord is the strength of my life, of whom shall I be afraid?"

Fear Him! For fear of the Lord is the beginning of knowledge. Enjoy the day!

Mash And Move Monday!

Psalm 27:2 – "When the wicked came against me to eat up my flesh, my enemies, and foes, they stumbled and fell."

Step on them or over them and keep moving toward the prize. Enjoy the day!

No Trepidation Tuesday!

Psalm 27:3 – "Though an army may encamp against me, my heart shall not fear."

Walk in courage and enjoy the day!

Whatever May Come, We Win Wednesday!

Psalm 27:3 – "Though war may rise against me, in this I will be confident."

Enjoy the day!

Totally Into Him Thursday!

Psalm 27:4 – "One thing I have desired of the Lord, that will I seek: That I may dwell in the house of the Lord all the days of my life..."

And He wants to dwell in our houses. Let Him in and enjoy the day!

Fabulous And Fine Friday!

Psalm 27:4 – "...to behold the beauty of the Lord and inquire in His temple."

We are an extension of His beauty so we may be examples for others to follow. In all your ways, be beautiful, and enjoy the day!

So Safe Saturday!

Psalm 27:5 – "For in the time of trouble He shall hide me in His pavilion..."

Share with somebody you know that there's a safe place where they can go, and it's in Him. Enjoy the day!

Shelter Me Sunday!

Psalm 27:5 – "In the secret place of His tabernacle, He shall hide me. He shall set me high upon a rock."

Hidden and still sittin' high. Glory! Enjoy the day!

ENJOY THE DAY, THIS WAY!

Mighty Monday!

Psalm 27:6 – *"And now my head shall be lifted up above my enemies all around me..."*

Be above yet stay grounded and pray for enemies and haters. Either they'll change, be removed, or be used with ALL other things that work together for our good. Enjoy the day!

Tune In, Turn Up Tuesday!

Psalm 27:6 – *"Therefore, I will offer sacrifices of joy in His tabernacle; I will sing, yes, I will sing praises to the Lord."*

Tune into the song that He places in your heart. Turn it up and have a joyful day!

Whispers In The Night Wednesday!

Psalm 27:7 – *"Hear, oh Lord, when I cry with my voice! Have mercy also upon me and answer me."*

Allow yourself to indulge in peaceful slumber, knowing that He hears you. Enjoy your restful night!

Something More Saturday!

Psalm 27:8 – "When You said, 'Seek My face,' my heart said to You, 'Your face, Lord, I will seek'."

The search for all we need and want begins and ends with Him. He's more than enough! Enjoy the day!

Show And Tell Sunday!

Psalm 27:9 – "Do not hide Your face from me; do not turn Your servant away in anger; You have been my help..."

Let's not talk about others and turn our backs, but let's show unconditional love and help. When they ask why we did it, we can tell them about our God who does it all. Enjoy the day!

Music In The Message Monday!

Psalm 27:9 – "Do not leave me nor forsake me, oh God of my salvation."

Al Green said, "Let's stay together." Chaka Khan simply and strongly said, "Stay!" Whatever your plea, know that He is our Main Ingredient; we are nothing without Him; and trust that He's (as Ronnie Laws or Incognito would put it) "Always there!" Enjoy the day!

Truth Be Told Tuesday!

Psalm 27:10 – "When my father and my mother forsake me, then the Lord will take care of me."

Those who birthed us may fail us. Forgive them, let it go, and let the Father to the fatherless in. You and what's best for you are always on His mind. Enjoy the day!

Worth Talking About Wednesday!

Psalm 27:11 – "Teach me Your way, oh Lord, and lead me in a smooth path, because of my enemies."

God's way confounds our enemies, so they talk about us. But really, they're just helping to tell our stories. Let them talk, walk your walk, and enjoy the day!

Tackle Our Thoughts Thursday!

Psalm 27:12 – "Do not deliver me to the will of my adversaries..."

Whatever His will, let's stay faithful and prayerful, knowing that it all works out for our good. Enjoy the day!

For You For Real Friday!

Psalm 27:12 – "For false witnesses have risen against me, and such as breathe out violence."

What does God say about you? Say what He says, speak life, and envision the moment when He anoints you in the presence of your enemies. Enjoy the day!

See It Before You Saw It Saturday!

Psalm 27:13 – "I would have lost heart, had I not believed that I would see the goodness of the Lord in the land of the living."

This too shall pass. Believe and see your change. Shout now and enjoy the day!

Surely, Surely Sunday!

Psalm 27:14 – "Wait on the Lord; be of good courage, and He shall strengthen your heart; wait, I say, on the Lord!"

Someone asked, "How long should we wait?" And the reply was, "Until your change comes!" 'Nuff said. Be patient and strong in the wait and enjoy the day!

ENJOY THE DAY, THIS WAY!

Holidays, Special Days And Events

Rev. Dr. Martin Luther King, Jr. Day

Moments With The "King" Monday!

Those who stand for nothing fall for anything. Rev. Dr. Martin Luther King, Jr. stood for something, which is why we celebrate this man who was worthy of a Noble Peace Prize for his vigilance and fight for equality. He has been given a day to be recognized and honored in song because he deserved it. (Thank you, Stevie.) Dr. King knew the King of kings, applied the power of prayer with action, and believed that change would come…and it did, albeit change is ongoing. Let us continue to rise and keep hope alive as we pay tribute to MLK. Enjoy the day!

Labor Day

Made For This Monday!

Many of us are glad to have been born and living in America. However, made in America ain't got nothing on being made and fashioned by the King, for the Kingdom, that God may get the glory! We were made to praise Him! Enjoy the day!

Election Day

To The Polls Tuesday!

How can our collective voices via action be heard? VOTE! It's a right that many fought and died for because our voices matter. Do your part, and VOTE! Enjoy the day!

Wounded Warriors Day

Wounded Warriors Day!

Let's thank our veterans for their service in protecting our country by extending a "thank you for what you do" or giving them a salute. May God bless all who have and those who are serving. Enjoy the day!

ENJOY THE DAY, THIS WAY!

Holiday Season, New Year,

Good Friday, And

Resurrection Sunday

(No special order of holiday events...just mindful words for the body, heart, and soul.)

Monday Morning Muse!

"A man's heart plans his way, but the Lord directs his steps."
— Proverbs 16:9

As we prepare to journey to other places or invite guests into our homes, pray for those traveling and those who may cancel, for only God sees the unforeseen when plans suddenly change. Enjoy the day!

Merry, Merry Monday!

The lights, the music, and all the charm and glamour of the holiday season are upon us. It's the most wonderful time of the year to share with others the real reason to be thankful and to tell what the season truly means to us. So, as you merrily go, let them know…and enjoy the day!

Milestone Monday!

When you run this life alone, you're in a race toward the finish line. When you run with God, He will give you grace to make it to the finish line. Make sure He's with you as you finish this year and pace yourself into the new year…gracefully. Our new beginnings are nothing without Him. Enjoy the day!

Take Time Tuesday!

Spend some time with yourself to reflect on the past year, identify and plan to correct what needs tweaking, and know that you get another chance to perfect it all in the new year. Reflect, correct, and perfect! Enjoy the day!

These Fine Men And Women Have Traversed Afar Tuesday!

Oh yes, we have! Over hills and mountains, through valleys and storms, standing on His promises while kneeling on our knees. Surely, the good has outweighed the bad – thank you, Lord. Let's commend and celebrate our resilience as we enjoy the day!

Today And Tomorrow Tuesday!

Plans don't have a past; they only have a present and a future. As the year ends, let's do as Paul instructs – forget what lies behind and press toward what lies ahead. It starts with a plan. Write the vision, make it plain, and run with it. Enjoy the day!

Timeless Treasures Tuesday!

Who cares what others think? If you like it, there's at least one someone who will love it! Put on that gaudy holiday brooch, necklace, cuff, or those flamboyant Christmas earrings you love, and enjoy the day!

Wonderful Almost Winter Wednesday!

Let the shopping begin! However, remember to shop wisely, be aware of your surroundings, and mindful not to walk away from your purse, wallet, children, and/or packages left in the cart. Enjoy the day and make it a safe and wonderful holiday shopping season!

Where Is The Love Wednesday!

The love is with us and in us, for it's the same love that saved us. He came, and we're better for it and glad about it. Celebrate Christ-mas and enjoy the day!

White As Snow Wednesday!

Jesus took on all sins – past, present, and future sins – so that we may be washed clean and forgiven when we receive Him as Savior. We celebrate His birth because He is, He came, and He gave the perfect gift – His life. Enjoy the season!

Toss It Up Thursday!

Toss what up? A salad! We all know Thanksgiving is coming. Hence, let's be proactive instead of reactive and eat lighter now; and if we overindulge at Thanksgiving dinner, it's okay – we've allowed for it in advance. Healthy lifestyles work and help you to enjoy each day!

Thanksgiving Thursday!

Indulge. Most of all, enjoy the holiday!

Top Of The Morning Thursday!

Time to update your holiday music collection? The list is plentiful! Here's two of my favorites: #1 – *The Jackson 5 Christmas* – (no home should be without this classic.) #2 – Kem's *What Christmas Means*. Share your holiday music favorites with someone and enjoy the day!

'Tis The Week Before Christmas Eve Thursday!

(Singing) "Give love on Christmas day. Oh, the man on the street and the couple upstairs all need to know there's someone who cares..." Let us be that "someone" helping others to enjoy the season, as God helps us to enjoy the day!

Fall Is Still Here And In Style Friday!

Frosty will have his day. For now, let's soak up this beautiful weather – it's perfect for people who love the autumn and winter fly, funky, and fresh fashions. Thank Him for the weather, and the coverings (the blood and the clothes), as you enjoy the day!

Favorite Things Friday! (It may not be Friday... but, it's Christmas!)

It's the most wonderful time of the year and one of my favorites. Yes, today we celebrate the birth of Jesus. Enjoy the day, and Merry Christmas!

Fired Up Friday!

Bringing one year to a close and beginning another excites me! Oh yes, we are overjoyed with the start of each new morning. However, knowing that He's kept and brought us through a consecutive 365 days and nights, and then brings those to a close only to bless and start us afresh on another year's journey should set our souls afire. Get ready, get fired up, and enjoy the day!

For Real Friday!

Jesus is real for real, and He wants to have a real relationship with you. In this new year, spend time with Him daily. He knows you better than you know yourself, so keep it real that He may draw nearer to you as you draw nearer to Him. Happy New Year and enjoy the day!

Sing Along Saturday!

It's the season that rings with music celebrating the birth of our Savior! Join in and enjoy the day!

Songs For Every Season Saturday!

Many know the holiday music, but do they know Him? Share with someone the good news about Jesus with hopes that they may desire more of Him in their life. As they grow in Him, they will find that He has songs for every season and in every key of life. His music helps us to enjoy the day!

Stop And Start Sunday!

In this final Sunday of the year, let's begin to mentally receive and accept that there are things we need to delete and things we need to add to our lives as we enter the new year. Stop the cycle that's left you with areas unfulfilled. Start a new cycle with a new perspective on life that begins and ends each day with Him, who holds the plan for your wonderful change. Know that it's never too late. Enjoy the day!

New Year's Eve! (For any day that's the last day of the year.)

This is it! Through it all, we made it to the last day of the year. Out with the old, in with the new, and be sure all hearts and minds are clear. No need to carry your worries

ENJOY THE DAY, THIS WAY!

and burdens into your new beginning. Release them to Him, who can give you a life story with a beautiful ending. Enjoy the day and have a safe New Year's Eve!

ENJOY THE DAY, THIS WAY!

Good Friday And Resurrection Sunday

Faithful Friend To The End Friday!

"Surely He took up our pain and bore our suffering, yet we considered Him punished by God, stricken by Him, and afflicted. But He was pierced for our transgressions, He was crushed for our iniquities; the punishment that brought us peace was on Him, and by His wounds we are healed." — Isaiah 53:4-5

There is no greater love. God bless you all and enjoy this Good Friday!

Surely, He Lives Sunday!

He came. He died. He took on all sin. He rose with all power and will come again. Jesus lives, and He saves. Happy Resurrection Sunday! Let's celebrate and worship our Savior as we break bread together and give thanks for what He did for us at Calvary. Enjoy the day!

ENJOY THE DAY, THIS WAY!

A Glimpse Of Black History Contributions And Quotes Series, Along With Valentine's Day Messages —

After all, it's February, y'all!

(FYI – Black History is also American History to be recognized and celebrated year-round!)

Muster Up Your Courage Monday!

"Grab the broom of anger and drive off the beast of fear."

~ Zora Neale Hurston

We have come this far by faith, even in times of fear, for our faith gave those before us the courage to stand side-by-side, facing white hoods and water hoses that couldn't wash our color nor us away. "Fear not, for I am with you", says the Lord. Enjoy Black History Month and make it a courageous day!

Mindful Of Morality Monday!

"Ability may get you to the top, but it takes character to keep you there." ~ Stevie Wonder

No matter what your worth in riches and gold, you can never buy a good reputation. Desire to have a name where people look forward to your entrance, not your exit, as you enjoy the day and Black History Month!

ENJOY THE DAY, THIS WAY!

Make It Easy On Yourself Monday!

"It's not the load that breaks you down; it's the way you carry it."

~ Lena Horne

When going through hard times, setbacks, and other challenges in life, it isn't necessary to show it so that everybody can know it. Walk, talk, and present yourself dignified with a holy humility that amazes others by how well you carry your cross as you encourage and lead by example on the way to your next victory. Chin up, and smile as you enjoy the day and Black History Month!

Motivation Monday!

"Most people fail in life not because they aim too high and miss, but because they aim too low and hit."

~ Les Brown

Our history is rich with stories of Black Americans who, despite their circumstances, achieved high levels of notable success worthy of mention in history books. Sadly, their stories were buried or hushed and never told. Let us resurrect the stories and share them with future generations so the pearls of positive history may touch, inspire, and remind them that overcoming and achieving is what we've done and continue to do. Enjoy the day and Black History Month!

Thanks For Mailing That Tuesday!

The letter mailbox, found on corners across this country, was invented and patented in 1891 by Philip B. Downing, a Black American. Prior to that, everyone had to take their mail to the post office. His invention made life easier for those the postmaster serves, and it created the need for new jobs. That's what God does for us. When we serve and dedicate our time to help make life better for others, He blesses us and opens windows of opportunity for the rest. "Black Power" fist up to the mailbox and enjoy this day in Black History Month!

What We Want For Them Wednesday!

"My hope for my children must be that they respond to the still, small voice of God in their own hearts."

~ Andrew Young

May the prayers of our ancestors continue to resonate within our prayers. May our children hear, recognize, and respond to His voice for their own good, and may healing and wholeness happen through His grace and mercy, for His namesake. Let Your still, soft voice drown out all the others, Lord. Amen. Enjoy the evening and Black History Month!

Wednesday Wake Up!

"Deal with yourself as an individual worthy of respect and make everyone else deal with you the same way."
~ Nikki Giovanni

People often give more respect to those they esteem over others. We are to treat everyone respectfully, for God is not a respecter of persons, nor should we be. Paul wrote (Galatians 2:6), "And from those who seemed to be influential (what they were makes no difference to me; God shows no partiality/favoritism) – those, I say, who seemed influential added nothing to me." God gives favor, not favoritism. Respect that you may be respected and enjoy the day and Black History Month!

Wise Words Wednesday!

"Prayer begins where human capacity ends."
~ Marian Anderson

Sooooooo true! Trying everything else and thinking we can fix problems or people on our own is not the answer. Pray – for God says, "I am That I Am." Whatever we need, imagine Him saying, "That I Am." Pray without ceasing, accept His divine intervention, keep trusting, and never let go. Enjoy the day and Black History Month!

"That's A Good Fit" Thursday!

Before the late 1800s, the maximum number of shoes handmade by an assembly of workers was seventy per day. Enter 1883 and Jan Matzeliger. This Black man invented and patented the "lasting machine" which increased production to seven hundred shoes per day. That's ten times more, y'all! He is the reason shoes can be mass-produced. Our mass producer is Jesus; He has a fit for all our needs and always leaves some overflow that we may give to others. We can't fill His shoes, but we can follow His lead…now that's a good fit. Enjoy the day and Black History Month!

That's A Good Move Thursday!

"I knew someone had to take the first step, and I made up my mind not to move."
~ Rosa Parks

Sometimes, the best move is no move. That's when we must stand and see the salvation, deliverance, yoke-breaking, mountain-moving, wall-removing power of the

Lord. Be still, knowing He is God, and make the mental move to enjoy the day and Black History Month!

Favor Love Friday!

"Hatred paralyzes life; love releases it. Hatred confuses life; love harmonizes it. Hatred darkens life; love illuminates it."
~ Martin Luther King, Jr.

God is love, and love always rules. Love always rules because God is King. Let's be inspired by love as we celebrate and enjoy each day of Black History Month!

Final Words Friday!

Katherine Dunham, an African American dancer, choreographer, and owner of one of the first Black ballet companies in the USA, once said, "I used to want the words 'She tried' on my tombstone; now I want 'She did it'." Whatever you're working on, know that God will give you help to complete the task. And when you reach the goal and utter, "It is finished", be not surprised when He replies, "Well done, my good and faithful servant." Enjoy the day and Black History Month!

Valentine's Day Messages

Sultry Soulful Sayings For Valentine's Day!

"Love makes your soul crawl out from its hiding place."

~ Zora Neale Hurston

Whether it's the love for your mate that makes your soul crawl out of its hidden places or the joy of curling up with your favorite book or movie, allow yourself to be carried away in the moment and make it a night, this Black History Month, that makes your soul never want to crawl back in! Here's to an enjoyable Valentine's Day!

Sweethearts And Valentine's Day!

"I have learned not to worry about love; but to honor its coming with all my heart." ~ Alice Walker

Still waiting for Mr. or Mrs. Right? Fret not. Focus and continue with God's plan for your life; and when love calls, you better answer! Keep your eyes on Him, and He will keep His eyes on the one He's preparing for you. God's plan is perfect, not a pick-any-card game. So, when the enemy puts some jokers in your path that look like the real thing, rebuke them and refocus your attention; God's mate for you is on the way. When they arrive, welcome and honor them, and they will do the same because that person was prepared just for you and you for them. Enjoy Valentine's Day and Black History Month!

ENJOY THE DAY, THIS WAY!

ENJOY THE DAY, THIS WAY!

Wise Words From Black Greek Letter Sorority And Fraternity Members Of The Divine Nine

ENJOY THE DAY, THIS WAY!

"Your life is not defined by the one place that you work."

~ Roland Martin, Alpha Phi Alpha

"Never be limited by other people's limited imaginations."

~ Dr. Mae Jemison, Alpha Kappa Alpha

"My work sometimes can be abstract and appear not to have direct relationship to African Americans' concerns, but in fact, it is based on that."

~ Donald Byrd, Kappa Alpha Psi

"As I learn from you, I guess you learn from me – although you're older – and white – and somewhat more free…"

~ Langston Hughes, Omega Psi Phi

"Service is the rent that you pay for room on this earth."

~ Shirley Chisholm, Delta Sigma Theta

"I think what motivates people is not great hate, but great love for other people."

~ Huey Newton, Phi Beta Sigma

"I will not wait for opportunities; I will create them."

~ Dionne Warwick, Zeta Phi Beta

"Release the negative vibe and let it go."

~ MC Lyte, Sigma Gamma Rho

"Blame is the coward's way out."

~ Elvin Hayes, Iota Phi Theta

Black Greek Letter Organizations are a part of Black History, and they continue to contribute and create new moments that will be chronicled in history books of the future. I hope you enjoyed this Black History Month series and that it has added to your enjoyment of Black History Month!

ENJOY THE DAY, THIS WAY!

About the Author

Patricia Wynn-Mason, a Philadelphia native, has always been a beacon of creativity. From her early years, she showcased an extraordinary talent for crafting melodies and lyrics, penning her first song while still in middle school. Her musical prowess continued to shine in college, where she composed a song for her sorority, that remains celebrated and sung worldwide.

Her journey of self-discovery led her to the telecommunications industry, where she began to fully realize the depth of her creative potential. Transitioning into the media industry as an advertising account executive, Patricia found a new canvas for her talents. She excelled in writing captivating commercials that resonated deeply with audiences, earning accolades for her ability to infuse wit, warmth, and emotion into her work. With a lifetime of nurturing her creative instincts, Patricia naturally gravitated towards literature. Her debut book, "Enjoy The Day, This Way", is a testament to her unique perspective on life. Blending humor, warmth, and profound insight, Patricia inspires readers to approach each day with optimism and gratitude.

As Patricia continues to inspire through her writing, she remains a testament to the power of creativity and resilience. Her story encourages us to explore our own creative potential, to find joy in the little things, and to live each day with a grateful heart. With her wisdom and experience, Patricia Wynn-Mason is not just an author, but a guide, showing us the way to a more fulfilling and joyful life.

DMX. "Party Up (Up in Here)." ...And Then There Was X, Ruff Ryders, Def Jam, 2000.

Kirk Franklin. "When I Think About Jesus". Whatcha Lookin' 4, GospoCentric Records, 1996.

Gloria Lynne. "I Wish You Love." Gloria Lynne, Everest, 1964.

Maxwell. "Whenever Wherever Whatever." Maxwell's Urban Hang Suite, Columbia, 1996.

Eve. "What Ya Want." Ryde or Die Vol. 1, Ruff Ryders Entertainment, 1999.

The Jackson 5. "Give Love on Christmas Day." Jackson 5 Christmas Album, Motown, 1970.

Kem. "What Christmas Means." What Christmas Means, Motown, 2012.

Roy Ayers. "Everybody Loves the Sunshine." Roy Ayers Ubiquity – Everybody Loves the Sunshine, Polydor Records, 1976.

Good Reads, "Myles Munroe > Quotes > Quotable Quote", 2024 Good Reads, accessed August 16, 2024

Lecrae. "Tell the World Feat. Mali Music." Lecrae Gravity, Reach, 2012.

SCRIPTURAL REFERENCES

All scripture quotations are sourced from
www.biblegateway.com
Specific translations are cited accordingly.

www.ingramcontent.com/pod-product-compliance
Lightning Source LLC
LaVergne TN
LVHW051951060526
838201LV00059B/3594